SNOWBOARDING

Philippa Perry

Illustrated by Rowan Clifford

Consultant: Tudor Thomas
Editor *Whitelines Magazine*

Hodder
Children's
Books
a division of Hodder Headline plc

Series design by Fiona Webb
Book design by Phil Crouch-Baker
Project Editor: Caroline Plaisted
Consultant: Tudor Thomas, editor *Whitelines Magazine*

Printed by Clays Ltd, St Ives plc.
Hodder Children's Books
a division of Hodder Headline plc
338 Euston Road
London NW1 3BH

Meet the author

Philippa Perry is a freelance writer and author who has written a handful of books for children. You may recognise her name from magazines or from her books *Olympic Gold*, *Mega Machines* and *Spooky Stories*. She's also written books about the police and the fire brigade for a series about teamwork, and *Activators: In-Line Skating*.

Philippa took up snowboarding three years ago when she realised that snowboarders seemed to have a lot more fun than skiers. She was amazed to find that snowboarding wasn't that hard to learn and was even more fun than it looked. She's done wing-walking, rock-climbing and bungee jumping and loves in-line skating around London.
Philippa would like to thank her friend Rachel for all her help with the book and her snowboard instructor Johnny for being the coolest teacher in the world.

Top Tip

If you come across a word or term you don't recognize, look it up in the glossary on page 123.

Introduction

If it's a beautiful day, with fresh, deep powder covering the mountains and blue sky above, then look carefully on the slopes, between the trees and at the top of the mountain and you're bound to see snowboarders. They'll be free-riding, doing aerials, pulling tricks, and basically having fun.

Snowboarding is the most exciting sport to hit the slopes for eons. But how do you get to be good? How do you ride with style? How do you perform tricks and jumps? What is the right gear to buy and where in the world do you go to learn? What are you waiting for? Read this book and get on board!

Philippe

Contents

1 Early riders   6

2 Getting on board   13

3 Ready to ride   27

4 More mountain manoeuvres   46

5 Up keep   65

6 Pipes, parks and big mountains   69

7 Getting tricky!   77

8 So you want to be a pro?   104

9 Sloping off   113

  Want to know more?   118

  Glossary   123

  Index   125

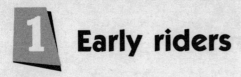

1 Early riders

The Dream

You're up before everyone else, on with your favourite beanie, you pick up your board and head out to catch the first lift. Free-riding from top to bottom with your mates, you catch some big air, session a McTwist and a 360 Air to Fakie in the half-pipe, and then it's over to the fun park to show some moves. You hook up with some new boarders at the mountain café and then spend the afternoon showing them around the back country.

Snowboarding is one of the fastest growing sports in the world. It's great fun, brilliant to do with friends, but best of all, unlike skiing, it's really easy to learn. In three days, with a few lessons, you could be riding in deep powder and having big fun with your mates. All you need is the right attitude, a bit of determination and skill, and of course, snow!

Early riders

You might think that snowboarding is something new but you'd be wrong.

In fact, people living in snowy, mountainous regions have been adapting the way they get about for hundreds of years, which meant all sorts of experiments with planks of wood strapped to people's boots. Nowadays, there are two main choices when you want to have fun on the mountain: snowboarding and skiing – and both sports have an equal number of fans.

Board bites

A short, wooden wide ski – possibly the most ancient snowboard in the world ever – was found left in a peat bog. It was thought to be over 4,500 years old. Some ancient rider is probably still wondering where he left it!

Although today snowboarding is a multi-million industry with manufacturers competing to bring out the latest and hottest gear every year, believe it or not, it all started back at school. In 1963, an American teenager called Tom Sims (who later became a snowboard legend as well as a world skateboard champion), designed a 'ski' board for a school project. Three years later he had perfected the board and the first snowboard was launched.

"IT'LL NEVER WORK SIMS, NEVER!"

"I DON'T KNOW. IT MIGHT JUST CATCH ON."

But while Tom was busy perfecting his board and being laughed at, another American called Sherman Poppen had the storming idea of surfing on snow and invented the 'snurfer board'. This was made out of a piece of plastic with a rope attached to the nose. Kids loved it and snurfing boards sold like hot cakes to surf, ski and skateboard fans.

Board bites

The first snurfing competition took place at Blackhouse Hill in Michigan in 1968. It was a hair-raising ride straight down hill. The winner was the first snurfer to cross the line in one piece!

Board bites

In the early years, it was surfers and skateboarders who wanted to recreate the feeling and attitude of their sport, who pushed snowboarding forward. When they were hanging out on holiday in the mountains they would take the trays from the mountain cafés and bars and slide about on them having fun.

In 1969, one of the most famous names in snowboarding, Jake Burton Carpenter, was given a snurfer for Christmas. This is how his passion for boarding began, and soon Burton began to make adaptations to his board so that is was more controllable. Soon, Burton Boards was born and Burton is now, along with Sims, one of the biggest names in snowboarding.

SNOW GO

Not everyone welcomed this new sport to the mountains. Sometimes for these early snowboarding pioneers, it felt like pushing a big snowball up hill. Some skiers and resorts felt that boarding was just a silly, dangerous fad that would soon disappear. People thought that snowboarders were reckless and a dangerous menace on the slopes. Boarders couldn't even use the slopes and pistes and had to hike off-piste to the mountain back country in the powder and soft snow.

"GO! NEVER DARKEN THIS PISTE AGAIN."

Today, snowboarding is an accepted sport. It has its own style as well as its own language and gear. There are snowboarding championships held all over the world for slalom, racing and freestyle, with top riders sponsored for large amounts of money.

Pro Talk

"I love all aspects of snowboarding. I don't compete for money, titles or prestige. I just love to ride for fun and for the sport."

Jasey Jay Andersen, Canadian champion snowboarder

SKIING VERSUS SNOWBOARDING

OK let's face it. Snowboarders and skiers are not the same. There is no doubt that there is, and has been, a rivalry between skiers and snowboarders. However, today, many snowboarders are also skiers and vice versa. There is much more friendliness between the two sports and both exist happily side-by-side on the slopes. You'll see people from 7 to 70 getting on board and hanging out.

Board bites

In 1998 Snowboarding was entered for the first time as an Olympic sport at the Winter Games in Japan. There were competitions in racing and freestyle.

WHY SNOWBOARDING IS BEST
(and why skiing isn't quite as great)

Snowboarding:

- It's really easy to learn – with lessons you can learn to snowboard in just three days. You'll be stopping, carving turns, performing simple jumps and riding even the steepest button lifts. And that's a fact!

- The equipment is much lighter and easier to carry. The boots are soft so that you can wear them comfortably around the resort.

- The clothes are things that you would happily wear at home.

- There's a friendliness between boarders. They say hello to each other and help each other on the slopes.

Skiing:

- It's a very hard sport to learn. It takes weeks to learn to parallel turn and years to get to a very high level where you can ski off-piste in deep powder.

- The equipment is heavy to carry and heavy to wear, especially the hard boots with their stiff shells. Your feet feel like squashed bananas if you try dancing or walking too far in ski boots in the resort.

- Most people wouldn't be seen dead in tight ski pants and jackets back home.

Getting on board

You don't need to be an extreme sports freak to board nor do you have to be particularly fit (although it does help give you a bit of a head start!). People of all ages can learn to board. Before you can hit the slopes or check out your local dry ski slope, you'll need to get the correct gear. This will not only protect you and keep you warm but it could save your life if you ever got into trouble or lost on the mountains.

Here's what you need:

JACKET

A loose jacket is important. It doesn't need to be particularly thick or heavy but it does need to be windproof and have a high neck to protect you against the elements out on the slopes. A longer tail or 'snow shirt', on the back of your jacket is a good idea because even the best boarders spend a lot of time sitting in the snow! Layering your clothes underneath the jacket is a brilliant idea because if you are hot you can take one of the layers off. Consider layers of a fleece, sweatshirt and a T-shirt.

BOARDING PANTS

These need to be loose fitting so that you can move easily. The best pants are made of Gore-tex™ material which is really strong, light and waterproof. Pants should be high-waisted and long enough at the bottom to cover the tops of your boots so that snow doesn't creep up your legs! Look for pants with reinforced bottoms and knees – snowboarders spend a lot of time on their bums and knees in the snow when they are learning!

GLOVES

These are really important because your hands come in contact with snow much more in snowboarding than skiing. Your gloves need to be made of a hard-wearing, waterproof material. Ideally they should extend above the wrist to keep out the snow. Some snowboard gloves have reinforced wrist protectors built in, but wrist bands for in-line skating work well too.

Board bites

In the first days of snowboarding, dayglo and flourescent colours were the in-thing. Apart from being horrible, these colours gave you a headache! Today, most snowboard gear is in earthy colours with cool designs.

SHADES AND GOGGLES

These are a must. The glare from the sun on the mountains can really damage your eyes. Even when the weather is overcast, UV rays can penetrate the clouds. Choose plastic lenses as glass ones can be dangerous. Goggles are really important for bad weather – they can help you see and protect your face from the biting wind and cold.

BEANIE AND NECK WARMER

There are thousands of beanies to choose from: from skull caps to over-the-top, brightly-coloured top hats. Whatever you go for, don't leave home without one, as they say! Neck warmers are really underrated. But if you don't want snow trickling down your neck, you know what to wear!

Sun sense

Always remember to protect your skin out in the sun and wind. Wear a lip salve and sunscreen protection with an SPF of at least 15. Remember: the higher the SPF number the longer your skin will be protected.

Suits you!

The type of board and boots you choose depends on the type of snowboarding you want to do. Soon after your first lessons (and the inevitable bruises!) you'll possibly want to buy your own equipment and may have an idea of what part of the sport you're interested in. Here are the different types of snowboarding styles you can choose from:

FREE-RIDING

As its name suggests, this is all about the freedom to explore the mountain and create your own style. With free-riding, you can combine all kinds of snowboarding disciplines, exploring all the different parts of the mountain off and on piste. This is the essence of the sport and the most exhilarating and fun, where snowboarders are still free spirits, exploring untracked slopes and deep powder under a blue sky.

SLALOM/GIANT SLALOM

Riders make tight, small turns or larger ones to negotiate a specially designed course, marked by poles, on a mountain slope.

HALF-PIPE

Just like skateboarders, half-pipe riders perform tricks in a specially-created half-pipe cut out of the snow. They perform jumps and airs above the lip of the pipe. The pipes are about 100 to 300 metres in length.

FREESTYLE

Even though half-pipe riding is a freestyle discipline, freestyle also covers riding on flat ground and doing jumps and tricks such as ollies, nollies, jibbing, bonking, and riding fakie. This is fun, dynamic and acrobatic, and probably requires the most skill. Freestyle riders tend to lead the way in tricks, clothes and attitudes.

Boards

Your instructor will be able to give you some advice about the best type of board for you. But here is the low-down on the basic board:

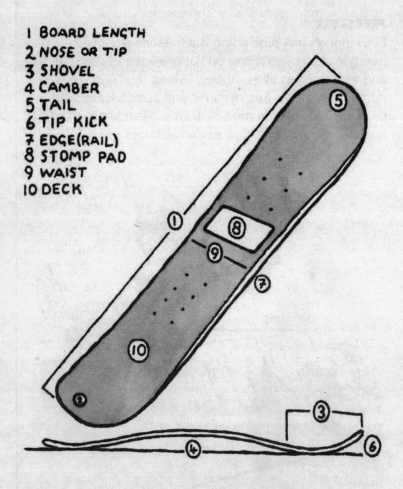

1 BOARD LENGTH
2 NOSE OR TIP
3 SHOVEL
4 CAMBER
5 TAIL
6 TIP KICK
7 EDGE (RAIL)
8 STOMP PAD
9 WAIST
10 DECK

Looking along the edge of the board, you can easily see that it is wider across the ends (shovels) and narrow in the middle. This "hour glass" shape is due to the "side cut".

18

And here are the different board variations:

FREESTYLE BOARD

These are quite flexible to enable the board to ollie, take off and land in absolute control. Freestyle boards have larger waists. They are longer and narrower than half-pipe boards and have more nose shovel and tail kick.

RACING AND ALPINE BOARDS

These have smaller noses and little or no tail kick as they are specially designed for hard-packed snow and require as much board as possible to be in contact with the snow.

FREE-RIDING BOARDS

These tend to be long and narrower than freestyle boards with more side radius. They have a longer nose shovel allowing them to maneouvre in deep snow.

HALF-PIPE BOARD

These are generally twin-tipped with each end basically the same size to perform tricks goofy and right-handed. They are shorter, fatter and lighter than other boards to help them take off in the pipe.

This board kicks!

There are loads of different makes of boards to choose from including K2, Burton, Sims, Forum, Generics, Airwalk, Morrow and loads more. There are boards for mountain trekking, for customising and racing. They come in all the colours of the rainbow from orange to black, with weird designs or plain finish.

Getting on board

Snowboard manufacturers are constantly competing to make the most radical, advanced snowboard ever. They sponsor professional boarders, produce clothing and trendy gimmicks and shades to give their equipment more appeal. Remember that no one board is better than another. The best way to find the right board for you is to read up reviews in snowboarding magazines and try them for size. No board will make you a fantastic boarder, only determination and skill. There's more advice on choosing what you need on page 24.

Board bites

Because boarders tend to spend so much time on their boards, and because they are so expensive, most fanatical boarders are completely in love with their snowboards and hate to be parted from them!

Putting the boot in

Now you've got to decide on the right board for you. For early riders this was easy as there was only one type of boot to wear! These days there are racks and racks of the things but don't be put off: once you've found the right pair for you, they can be heat moulded to your feet and you'll never feel like taking them off again!

FREESTYLE AND FREE-RIDE BOOTS

These boots are soft, allowing for masses of flexibility to perform tricks and ollies.

ALPINE OR RACING

These are hard and a bit like traditional ski boots. They give maximum protection to the feet and ankles for racing and fast carving. They also give maximum stability and control at high speeds.

What a bind up

There is a bit of history attached to bindings that is worth knowing. When the snowboard was originally invented, it was designed to provide a winter alternative to skateboarding. Therefore, the original binding – to keep the sport as near to skateboarding and as challenging as skateboarding – was never supposed to be more than something to hold the foot in place on the board. Many snowboarders feel that soft bindings are nearer to the true ideals of the sport. But as snowboarding grows, the technology of bindings is constantly advancing, much the same as ski bindings seem to be improved from year to year.

Getting on board

So, do you go for old-style strap bindings or the relatively new clicker or step-in bindings that were first seen on the slopes in 1996. It's a wonder anyone ever makes it out of the shops on to the slopes at all! Here's a look at the pros and cons of both types of bindings:

STRAP BINDINGS

These are also called soft bindings. They have a high back to the heel and two straps over the foot and ankle.

Pros: You can easily get in and out of these by unlocking or locking them with the straps. They are safe and won't spring open unexpectedly and any packed snow that might get caught in them is easily removed. You can wear a soft boot that is comfortable enough to wear around the house or for après ski. Soft bindings are preferred by most free-stylers.

Cons: You have to sit down on the snow to do them up. They take longer to get in and out of than step-ins or clickers.

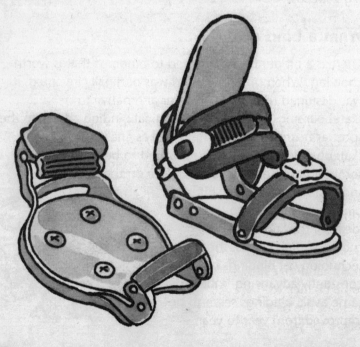

CLICKERS OR STEP-IN BINDINGS

These are similar to traditional soft bindings except there are no straps over the foot. You get into them by placing your toe in first and then clicking down with your heel. Step-ins offer more support than conventional bindings and therefore aren't as flexible. Because they are easy to use, beginners often prefer step-ins.

Pros: You can just step into these. You don't need to sit on the wet snow to do them up. They offer a bit more edge control and feedback than soft bindings.

Cons: Snow can get caught in the grooves which makes it difficult to click in properly. The bottom of the boot has a hard metal plate which makes the boots heavier and less comfy.

As you can see, there are disadvantages and advantages to both types. If you're not sure which will suit you, why not try out a set from a local ski rental shop next time you are on the mountain?

Spenny!

There are no two ways around it, snowboarding is an expensive sport! The complete kit for snowboarding will set you back some serious cash – and that's before you've even glimpsed the snow!

But don't worry, you can rent or borrow gear for your first lessons which will help you to get a feel for the equipment and the basic moves and give you a chance to suss out the best set-up for you.

"Ooh Sir does look 'Rad' everyone will be wearing it!"

The top tips for buying new gear

- Always buy from a specialist shop. Department stores and discount shops are not the best places to buy equipment.

- Ask the assistants for their advice on the board and boots for you. They are probably snowboarders themselves.

- Track down the stores that do package deals on boards, boots and bindings for lower prices.

- Consider buying by mail order to get good prices but try the gear on in a shop first!

- The snowboarding magazines (see page 120) are brilliant places for checking out new gear and prices. You may find ads for ex-demo gear or sponsors used stuff which is worth taking a look at.

- Ask the advice of an experienced snowboarder or your instructor about what worked for them when they were starting out.

- If you buy second-hand, make sure you check the state of the board: Are the sides and edges cracked? Is the top or base damaged? What about the tail and nose? Are the bindings cracked or damaged?

- Avoid second-hand boots as these won't mould to your feet. Remember that the boots are the link between you and the board so they've got to be right.

- Don't be duped into buying something you're not happy with – whatever the sales assistant says! If you're not happy, go to another shop.

Getting it on

So you've decided which type of boarding's for you, you've got the look you want and your board, boots and bindings. Before you set off and book a holiday, it might be a good idea to check out a local dry or artificial ski and snowboarding slope. This is the place to learn, and meet other snowboarders on special snowboard evenings and club nights. If it's a good centre, you should be able to get all the advice you need.

Artificial or dry slopes are made from a material called Dendex which is basically a series of nylon brushes, meshed together in a pattern that looks like chicken wire. Yup, you've guessed it – falling on Dendex really hurts and it's easy to catch your finger in, so make sure you've got lots of protective gear and padding on before you try a dry slope.

The slopes aren't very long, but just long enough to have a few goes at turning. One advantage is that you'll be able to get some practice getting on and off lifts, which is one of the hardest things to learn as a snowboarder. You'll also avoid embarrassing first moments on the mountains! There are details of artificial ski slopes on page 118.

Board bites

Boarding on a dry slope is nothing like the same feeling that you get on the mountain. If you can afford to go straight to a mountain and to persuade your parents to mortgage the house, your Gran, the dog, the car ... anything ... in order to have the best holiday of your life, then try. If not, it's off to the wiry carpet, I'm afraid.

Get this!

Apart from the obvious equipment we've already talked about, there are lots of other things that you should have for your first and subsequent snowboarding outings:

SUNSCREEN:

A must! At high altitudes on mountain tops, the air is thinner and the sun burns quicker. It's important to use a high factor sunscreen of SPF15 or more. Make sure it's waterproof, sweatproof and rub proof.

STOMP PADS:

These are for the back of your board for resting your boot on while you're negotiating the lifts. They come in all shapes, sizes, and designs.

POWER STRAPS AND HEEL ANCHORS:

These give extra support to the heel and boot by tying round the top of the boot and around the heel to hold it firmly in place.

MINI TOOL KIT:

Essential to have with you at all times. Bindings do come loose and if you've got your tool kit on you, you can tighten up the screws without having to hike back down the mountain in your boots!

BOARD LOCK:

This will protect your board from theft while you are resting or in the mountain bar. You can lock up a few boards with one lock if you are with your mates.

BACK PACKS AND BOARD BAGS:

Great for carrying your gear to and from the resort and for keeping essential items (fleece, goggles, sunscreen) handy if you are on a hike off piste, looking for 'freshies', or untracked areas.

3 Ready to ride

You've got your wrap-around Oakleys, the baggy look and your favourite beanie on your head. Let's face it, you're stoked! You're finally ready to ride!

Go to school

In this chapter, we're going to look at the first basic moves you will need to get you started. It's a good idea to take lessons – you won't need many, but a couple of days at snowboard academy will mean you'll progress much more quickly and won't pick up any bad habits. You also need to think of the safety issue: mountains can be really dangerous places and if you don't know how to stop and slide then you could be careering downhill out of control, hurting yourself and others.

Ready to ride

Whether you are taking lessons at the local dry slope or at a mountain ski school, you'll get the chance to meet other learners who'll give you encouragement and swap tales of enormous bruises and wipe-outs and generally have a laugh. You'll also meet friends whom you can board with when you're ready to take off on your own.

But the best things about snowboard school is the instructors. They won't be like any other teachers you've ever met before. All snowboarding instructors are mad about snowboarding and that's why they teach it, so that they get to hang out in the mountains for half a year and get paid for it too. They're cool, laid back, young, fun, and mad about boarding and encouraging.

Board bites

If you have a few lessons, you can learn to snowboard to a level where you can have fun safely in about three days.

How to spot your instructor

Snowboard instructors are very different from ski instructors. Here's a guide to spotting your snowboard instructor compared to a ski instructor on your first day.

"You are late!"

"Hey Dude, how's it hanging?"

Snowboard instructor

1 Your teacher will probably turn up looking as if he's just rolled out of bed.

2 He'll greet you with a big smile, a high five and possibly "Yo dude".

3 Lessons won't be in straight lines but higgledypiggly circles.

4 He'll keep telling you how fantastic snowboarding is and about all the brilliant places to ride on the mountain.

5 When you wipe out he'll congratulate you and have a laugh with you, after checking that you're OK.

6 He'll love drinking hot chocolate with you, looking at the mountain and sharing your sweets.

Ski instructor

1 He's always neat and tidy in a clean, tight, regulation suit.

2 He'll greet you with a cursory nod and tell you to stand in line in order of height and age and take the registration in the morning.

3 Lessons are always in straight lines.

4 He'll be terrifyingly good at skiing and will make you feel like you're completely useless.

5 When you fall over he'll send you to the back of the class.

6 At the end of the lessons, he'll be off to join the other teachers in the staff room to moan about you.

The first day

Here are some tips which will make you feel more confident on the slopes on your first day:

BOARD SAFETY

Carry your board the correct way with the safety strap tied round your arm and your back supporting your board. This will stop your board careering off down the mountain.

An out of control board is lethal. Be careful when you're on the mountain side to turn your board upside down so that the bindings are digging into the snow. This will stop it from sliding away from you.

AND REACH, TWO, THREE, FOUR

It's really important to warm up every morning before you go snowboarding. If you do some stretching exercises before you take to the slopes, you won't pull muscles or strain yourself snowboarding and end up resting the next day with a cup of cocoa like a granny!

NECK

BOTTOM
(OOH-ERR)
AND THIGHS

SHOULDERS

BACK

HAMSTRING

31

ARE YOU GOOFY?

No, it's nothing to do with the famous cartoon dog! Goofy basically means that you ride with your right foot forward on the board. Most people (70%) are regular, which means they ride with their left foot forward on the board. If you've ever surfed or skateboarded, you should know which foot you prefer to have forward. But, if not, here's a simple way to find out. Imagine you're sliding about with your mates on the freshly waxed floor of the school hall in your socks, which foot would you naturally put forward? Don't worry if you're not sure, once you're up and riding you can change your position easily.

Basic riding position

Before you ride, you'll need to know the basic riding position. This is really important because if you are in the right riding position, you should get on much more quickly.

1 Your body weight should be forward over your front foot.
2 Bend at your knees, not your waist.
3 Always keep your back straight and vertical, your head up and eyes looking forward.
4 Use your arms for balance. To begin with, they can be outstretched in front of you.
5 Stand parallel with the board, then turn your hips, shoulders, and head slightly across the board to face the way you are going.
6 Relax! Being stiff and tense will make snowboarding more difficult.

Top Tip

Make sure you wear some thermal leggings on your first few days of learning to snowboard as you'll probably spend quite a lot of time sitting on your bum in the snow!

Top Tip

A good exercise is to practice moving from a position facing forward with your board horizontal across the mountain to the riding position. Your body weight should be forward over your front foot and your arms out in front of you. Try this a few times until you can do it smoothly and naturally.

Strapping in

You've got your board, you've warmed up and you're ready to strap into your bindings for the first time.

1 Find a section of flat, soft-packed snow on a nursery slope or near the bottom of the mountain.
2 Sit down, holding on to your board carefully, and tie the safety strap to your front leg, before putting the board down on the snow.
3 Buckle your front foot into the binding, making sure you've cleared away any ice or snow caught in your bindings or on the bottom of your boot.
4 When fastening your bindings, begin with the ankle strap, then the toe straps. (If you have a step-in or clicker bindings, step into the binding with the toe first and then click in the heel of your boot.)

Fall guys

Face it: you're going to fall over when you're learning! The parts of your body that take the most knocks when you're boarding are your wrists, bottom, and knees. The best way to avoid serious injuries is to learn how to fall properly.

1 When falling forwards, whatever you do, don't use your hands to stop yourself. Clench your fist and put your arms out in front of you, and try to fall on your forearms.

2 When you're learning you could wear knee pads on the inside of your baggy trousers to protect your knees. Some snowboard pants come with knee padding already fitted.

3 If you fall backwards, you're going to land on your bum, but make sure you don't tense up. You could try padding your bottom with a cushion to make the fall a bit softer!

Board bites

Sprained and broken wrists are the most common snowboard injuries. 35% of all injuries happen to learner snowboarders.

What's what on the snowboard

We've already looked at the basic board on page 18, but here's a more detailed guide to what's what on your board. Use it to refer to as you go through the book so that when you read "Put your weight on the toe edge", you'll know what we're talking about!

SNOWBOARDER

Back shoulder   Front shoulder

Smile

Back hand

Front hand

Back foot

Front foot

Tail   Tip (nose)

SNOWBOARD

Heel edge (under heels)   Toe edge (under toes)

Getting your balance

Here are some exercises to help you get the feel for the board:

SKATING PRACTICE

With your front foot in the binding only, choose a flat area and skate around using your back foot to push off as if you were on a skateboard. When you are moving along, place your back foot on the stomp pad to get the feeling of riding a snowboard. As you get more confident, practice skating the board for as long as you can before you have to put your back foot down.

Top Tip

While you're practising these exercises, you don't need to take your board off. You can walk your board back up the slope by digging in the toe edge of the board in the snow and dragging it up the hill in a horizontal position.

WALKING THE BOARD

A good exercise is to try walking the board round in a circle, dragging the board behind you and controlling it.

FROG HOPPING

You can hop like a frog with your arms out in front of you on the snow and pulling your knees up. This is good for getting out of deep snow quickly.

STANDING UP

When the snow is deep it is easier to
stand up on your toe edge rather
than your heel edge which might
make you slip down the mountain.

To stand up
on your heel
edge, pull your snowboard close to
your body and dig the heel edge in
the snow. Reach across and grab the
toe edge with your hand. Now pull
yourself up using your hands and
straightening your legs.

TOE-SIDE TURN

Try a toe-side turn
with the front foot in
the binding. Turn to
the right if regular and
to the left if you're
goofy. You do this by
turning your upper
body in a direction up
the mountain while
putting pressure on
your toe edge and
gently lifting your
heels.

HEEL-SIDE TURN

Now try turning in the opposite direction. Push off down a
slight slope and glide. As you near the bottom, keep your
weight over your front foot and turn your upper body in the
direction you want to go, keeping your arms out in front of
you all the time and in the direction you want to go.

Strapped in

Now it's time to strap both feet in. These exercises are designed to make you feel comfortable with the board strapped on your feet and on the flat.

1 Jump up and down on the spot and try turning the board 90%. Make sure you bend your knees when you land.
2 Rock your board from side to side like a seesaw, to feel the limits of your board. Lean forward and backwards as far as you can go without falling.

Pro talk

"Skateboarding is a very good alternative to snowboarding. Skateboarding can help a lot in getting the strength, balance and technique you need for snowboarding."

Micki Albin, Swiss rider

Quick quiz

Let's test the snowboarding knowledge you've learned so far to see how you are getting on.

1 What are clickers?
   a) musical instruments b) type of bindings c) shoes

2 What is a snurfer?
   a) an early kind of snowboard b) a sort of elf or pixie
   c) a mountain slope

3 What did early snowboarders use to skate about on?
   a) plastic bags b) big books c) café trays

4 What is the surface of a dry slope made of?
   a) carpet b) Dendex c) Gore-tex™

5 What is a stomp pad?
   a) a dance b) a flat c) a pad on your board for your feet

The scores:

1	a) 0	b) 2	c) 1
2	a) 2	b) 1	c) 0
3	a) 1	b) 0	c) 2
4	a) 1	b) 2	c) 0
5	a) 1	b) 0	c) 2

Total:

7-10: You're well on your way to being a brilliant snowboarder. Everything seems to come naturally to you and you'll be free-riding in deep powder in no time at all.

4-7: You've got a bit of way to go yet. You're not quite sure about this sport, and don't know how to relax yet.

0-3: You're hopeless case. You may as well stay in bed!

Well, it's back to the basic moves. The next four moves are really important, as they form the basics you'll need to move on to faster turns, carving and jumping.

SIDESLIP: TOE EDGE

This is the equivalent of the skiers snow-plough. Your weight should be distributed 50/50 on both feet. With your knees bent and ankles and hips relaxed, slide, keeping the board 90% to the slope (ie horizontal across the slope). Control your speed and practice stopping by putting pressure on your toes and lifting your heels.

SIDESLIP: HEEL EDGE

Once you've got the hang of sideslipping on the toe edge, it's time to try the heel edge. Start by sitting facing down the slope with your heel edge horizontal across the slope. Try standing up. Once you're up (which isn't easy), keep your arms out in front of you, and start sliding keeping your weight over both feet. You can control your speed by putting more pressure onto your heels and lifting your toes.

TRAVERSING

Once you can slide slip both heelside and toeside, you should try a side slip across the slope in a traversing movement. Do this by moving your body weight over your front foot so that there is more pressure on your front foot than on your back foot. To stop, move your weight back equally over both feet. Now try leading with the back foot (ie traversing fakie or backwards).

FALLING LEAF EXERCISE

This gets its name from the fact that if you are doing it right, the movement you make will be similar to that of a leaf falling from a tree, falling this way and that. Follow the same movements as if you were traversing the slope. Immediately move your weight to the back foot and then to the front foot again. This is an excellent move for when you need to negotiate rocks or groups of people in crowded areas.

PRACTISING HALF TURNS

Before you try a full turn, it's a good idea to try half a turn to get the correct position and to make sure that you are able to control the speed of your turn.

1 From a side slipping position on your toe edge, put nearly all of your weight over your front foot and turn your upper body towards the nose of the board.

2 As the nose of the board moves down the mountain, lower your centre of gravity by bending your knees. This helps to put pressure on the toe edge.

3 Now turn your body up the hill, while sliding the back foot down the hill putting pressure on your toes.

Next try to do a half turn on the heel edge.

1 From a slide slipping position on the heel edge, shift most of your weights over the front foot, keeping your upper body facing down the slope.

2 As the nose of the board begins to slide down the mountain, bend your knees to lower your centre of gravity. This will help you to put pressure on the heel edge.

3 Keeping your weight over your front foot, turn your upper body in the direction you are doing.

43

What a drag

Just when you thought you were really getting the hang of things, the drag lifts and chair-lifts have to be negotiated. The truth is they're not really as bad as they look. You just need to watch out and use a bit of common sense. The different types of lifts include buttons, T-bars, rope tows and chair lifts of different kinds.

NEGOTIATING A T-BAR OR BUTTON LIFT

1   Approach the lift with the front foot in the binding and back foot pushing you along. This is when the skating movement that you learnt before will come in handy.

2   Once in position to take the button, flex a bit at the knees and relax. Place the button between your legs, and as you move off lean back slightly. If you lean too far forward, you will fall off and get dumped in front of laughing skiers – which you don't want!

3   As soon as you receive the button, place your back foot on the pad between the bindings and keep your board as flat as possible so that you don't catch an edge or get caught off balance. Keep your weight between the bindings when riding up the lift and remember to stay low.

44

4   Once you get to the top make
    sure that none of your
    clothing is caught on the
    button or T-bar. Use the
    sliding and skating exercise to
    move quickly out of the way
    and make sure you avoid
    groups of people that may be
    standing around waiting at
    the top of the lift. If you need
    to stop very quickly to avoid
    trouble, just sit down in the
    snow. It's not that cool, but it's
    much better than smashing
    into a group of dosey skiers.

Don't worry if you fall off the first time – it happens to
everyone. The first few times you use a chair lift, you can
carry your board as long as you keep the strap carefully tied
around your arm.

Once you're ready to use the chair lift with your board on
your feet, remember to
use the sliding and
skating movements to
get on and off. Don't get
your clothes or binding
caught in the chair lift. As
you glide away from the
lift, keep your weight
forward all the time. If
you lean backward, you'll
just shoot off across the
piste. Don't take your
back foot off the pad or
you'll fall over.

4 More mountain manoeuvres

Before we get on the hard stuff (turns, carving, jumps and ollies), it's time to check out the rules of the mountain. Mountains can be very dangerous places. Even on a sunny day, the weather can change in a flash and clouds and mist come in obscuring the slopes and making it difficult to see more than a few feet in front of you. If you are off piste, then this will be even more hazardous.

Be board smart

1 Always stop and look when you come to a cross-road with another slope. If you were on a road you'd never walk straight over without looking. The same rule applies to a mountain slope.

2 As the snowboarder coming from behind, you are always responsible for any collisions, so keep your eye on the person in front of you. If they are out of control and weaving in and out, it is best to avoid them. They may have drunk too much 'vin chaud' or are simply beginners.

3 If you need to sit down, don't sit in the middle of the piste. It may seem like common sense, but a skier coming down the mountain at break-neck speed may find it hard to stop quickly and may not be looking where he's going anyway. Always sit at the side of the slope. You can take in the view better here too!

4 Don't ski off piste if you are a beginner unless you are with an expert or a snowboard instructor who knows the mountain really well. There is no better feeling than boarding off piste in deep powder, but getting caught in a whiteout is not much fun.

5 Always obey the instructions and signs on the mountain. If a slope is in danger of avalanches, make sure you don't got there!

6 If you are hiking off piste, always wear a 'pieps' or avalanche transiever, so that if you do get caught in a dangerous situation, rescuers can find you.

7 Take a guide with you whenever possible.

So that's the serious stuff. The truth is that many people snowboard because they're not like skiers, content to potter around the pistes. They're in the mountains to ride and live life to the max. Go ahead and try some jumps, but always be safe whatever you do. Know your limits and have fun! Still, you don't have to go this far ...

On the turn

It's now time to start learning how to turn. To complete a basic turn you'll have to combine all the things you've learnt so far. Before you start practising turns, make sure you choose a place that isn't too congested with skiers and snowboarders.

Top turning tips

1 Keep your head up all the time and your arms outstretched for balance.

2 Your head, arms, shoulders and hips should move in the direction of the turn.

3 Keep your knees bent all the time.

4 Make sure most of your weight (80%) is over your front foot as you turn.

5 Extend your body upwards as you turn to change edge pressure during the turn.

TOE-SIDE TURN

1 Start with the side-slipping position on the heel-side edge with your weight evenly over both feet.

2 Now move most of your weight to your front leg.

3 The nose of the board will begin to fall down the slope. As it does, keep your weight on the front foot and allow the back to glide for an instant.

4 Once the board is gliding down the slope on its base, transfer the pressure to the toe-edge, while keeping the weight on the front foot. Make sure you don't lean back or the board will shoot out in front of you.

5 As you begin to turn, use your upper body to help you by turning your hips, shoulders and arms. This will help turn the board.

49

More mountain manoeuvres

HEEL-SIDE TURN

1 Starting from the side slipping position on the toe-side edge, keep your weight distributed evenly over both feet and move down the slope.

2 Move most of your weight onto your front leg, putting pressure on your front foot.

3 The nose of the board will start to move down the slope, as it does, maintain the weight over the front foot and allow the board to leave the edge and glide on its base. The straight line down the mountain which the board falls along when it is flat on the slope is called the fall line. There's a bit about the fall line below.

4 As the board is gliding, transfer pressure to the heel edge and lift up your toes, keeping your weight on the front foot. Make sure you don't lean back at this stage.

5 As you put pressure on your heel edge, use your upper body to help in the turning process, keeping your arms out in front of you. At the same time, slide your back foot down the hill.

Board bites

This turn is much more difficult than the toe-side turn. Make sure you don't swing your body and don't lean back.

Pro talk

"If you have trouble remembering to bend and rise in the turn, it can help to imagine you are a midget when you're turning and traversing and a giant when you're getting ready for the next turn!"

Hilary Maybery, former-USA National Champion

The fall line

If you drop a ball down a mountain, it will fall straight down. This is called the fall line. Just like the ball, if you stand up on your board so that the pressure is off the edges, you will move naturally down the fall line.

You can see how to use the fall line to control your speed by turning across it to slow down.

Linking turns

Now you can perform these basic turns, it's time to link them together!

As you begin to make each turn from the side-slipping position, lower your centre of gravity by bending your knees. This adds more power to the turn by making the edge grip more effectively in the snow. At the end of this movement, you'll need to stand up again slightly in order to take the weight off the turning edge ready to turn on the other edge.

Top Tip

Try to reduce the length of time that you spend on the traverse between your turns. This will give you more confidence and stop you from getting in the way of other snowboarders and skiers.

Board bites

The best way to get good at turning is to practise a lot. Don't be afraid to link turns together and to try steeper slopes. While you're practising your turns, make sure you choose a good wide open slope with few people. Don't practice turning in a mogul field.

Top tips for turning

1 The board will fall quite quickly if you're turning properly. Don't panic and lean back or the board will move even faster. Keep your weight on the front foot so that you can control it more easily, and you shouldn't have any problems.

2 Don't swing your body when you're turning. This is a common mistake to make but hard to shake if you get into the habit.

Picking up speed

Now it's time to get more speed into your turns, to make smaller turns, and to look like a pro.

TURNING IT ON

1 Start by side-slipping on to the heel-side edge and transfer most of your weight on to your front foot to the riding position as in a basic turn.

2 As the board starts to turn quickly, bend at the knees, and allow the front of the board to turn until the front of the board is flat on the snow and you are off the heel edge.

3 Put more weight on your toes and slightly lift your heels and bend your knees. You should now be going faster. At the same time, turn your shoulders and hips in the direction you are going.

4 You should now find yourself crossing the toe-edge side. Now, build up some speed by transferring most of your weight to your front foot. Start to turn by bending your knees and leaning your shoulders in the direction you want to go. Put pressure on the heel edge by lifting up your toes slightly and bending your knees.

Top tips for turning

1 Always look where you're going and make sure you have plenty of slope space to make your turn.
2 It's easier to make intermediate turns if you're moving fast. So don't be afraid to rage!

Pro talk

"Always try to stay relaxed when you're snowboarding. Stay lose and the feel what your body is doing. That way you'll have a lot more fun!"

Lowell Hart from American Snowboard Academy

Ride some grass

Some boarders don't let the fact there's no snow on the ground bother them. Eleven-year-old Colum Mytton from North Yorkshire is so boarding barmy that he actually rides the grassy hills of the Pennine Mountains behind his house. He just points himself down the hill and goes for it!

Cranking it up

You're now ready to try some basic free-riding skills. Free-riding is really what snowboarding is all about – it's you on your own or with some mates on the mountain slopes, taking off for somewhere and doing something because it feels good. There are no judges, teachers, clocks or gates, no signs and no problems. You can carve the hard snow, surf powder, jump over bumps or moguls and just ride free.

CARVING IT

Not the Sunday roast! This kind of carving is one of the best feelings you can get when you start to learn to snowboard. Carving takes the intermediate turn a stage further. Instead of sliding the board across the slope, the edge digs into the packed snow leaving a razor edge track in the snow. Here's how you do it:

1 Build up a bit of speed by crossing the slope on a toeside turn. Transfer your weight mostly to the front foot and turn your leading shoulder and hip in the direction you want to go.

2 Begin to bend at the knees, and put more weight over the heel edge. This will put pressure on the heelside edge and the board will immediately change from the toeside edge to the heel edge.

Top tips for carving

1 The key to carving is that the board should never be flat on the snow, but switching immediately from one edge to another.
2 Keep your centre of gravity low by bending your knees and keeping your knees closer together.
3 Whilst your knees are bent, the upper part of your body should be straight.

Board bites

If you lean all the way over so that you can touch the snow, you'll be doing what is called the Eurocarve. This is when the edge of the board is so angled that you can touch the snow with your hands. The Eurocarve is also known as the Vitelli Turn, after the French dude who invented it – Serge Vitelli. He was so good they named two more after him too!

57

Air raising

Now it's really time to turn up the volume! This is the bit you've been waiting for. The bit where you put some blue air between the bottom of the board and the mountain. The bit where you're parents start praying and your friends gasp in amazement. This joint's really jumping!

For your first flight through the air, it's best not to try anything too risky. The key to jumping is landing. It doesn't matter how high you jump, it's landing that counts. If you can't land then don't bother to take off. Here's how:

1   Choose a small jump with a smooth and gentle landing.
2   Practise going over the jump without leaping to get a feel for the slope and where you're going to end up. When you feel a bit more confident, approach the jump a bit faster and ollie (see below) when you get to the top. Make sure your board is not on an edge when you take off or you'll be unbalanced in the air. When you get better, try adding some 'grabs' or hand tricks when you're in the air.

Ollieing

1 The basic jump that will help you to get some big air is the 'ollie', which is very similar to a skateboard ollie. Begin moving in a straight line. Rock all your weight onto your back foot. Jump forward and up and off the tail of your board.

2 Balance yourself in the air with your arms. as you land, make sure your base goes down as flat as possible. Keep your knees bent as you land and your arms out for balance.

3 You've done it!

How does this grab you?

Once you've perfected the basic ollie, it's time to add some grabs! Here's some favourites.

CHICKEN SALAD: with your front hand, grab the heel edge of the board between your legs.

INDIE: with your back hand, grab the toe edge of your board between your legs.

METHOD: your front hand grabs your heel edge between your feet.

MUTE: grab your toe edge with your front hand between your feet.

DOING A BONE: grab the nose of the board with your front hand and lean towards it like this boarder is doing here:

Board bites

The Nollie jump is just like an ollie but you take off from the nose of the board rather than the tail.

FAKING OR SWITCHING IT

Riding fakie is riding backwards or tail first. This is an easy freestyle trick that you should try to perfect before you move on to more advanced trickery! Watch any good snowboarder and you'll probably not be able to tell if they're goofy or regular because they look so relaxed riding in both directions.

Fakie tips:

1 Always look in the direction you want to go and make sure there are no people or obstacles in your way.
2 Keep your weight centred and don't lean too far forward.

Pro talk

"When I started riding in 1998, I didn't even care if the sport would get bigger, I just enjoyed riding. I think it has grown so much because the lifestyle appeals to young people as much as the sport."

Sigi Grabner, Champion snowboarder from Austria

BONKING

Here's something to really impress your mates. Bonking is stylish and fun and is guaranteed to get you noticed. And no, it's not something you get arrested for! When you're jumping over an obstacle or passing a box or getting ready to get off a rail or bench, just slap it with your board. Push your leg down and hit the object, then lift off again. If you hit something with the front of your board, it's a nose bonk and if you use the back it's a tail bonk. Happy slapping!

Snowboard speak quiz

OK so you're about half way through the book now. You've got the gear, you've got the look, but do you really know your shifties from your aerials? Try our quick quiz to test your snowboard speak.

1 What is a goofy?
   a) a cartoon dog
   b) someone who's useless at parties
   c) a boarder who rides right foot forward

2 What does 'spinning frontside' mean?
   a) turning the same way as a heelside turn
   b) spinning on your head in the snow
   c) spinning on the tip of your board

3 What's a duckfoot?
   a) a lucky mascot
   b) where feet are angled out in opposite directions
   c) a type of snow boot

4 What's boning?
   a) feeling stoked
   b) pushing yourself to the limit
   c) fully extending one or both legs

5 What's the rail on a snowboard?
   a) the side
   b) the place where you put your feet
   c) a place to rest your hot chocolate

6 What's a bunny slope?
   a) a very easy slope for beginners
   b) a place where rabbits hang out
   c) a very difficult slope with lots of jumps

7 Which of these is not a half pipe move?
   a) alley oop
   b) stale burger
   c) indy air

8 Which of these would you not find in a half-pipe?
   a) transition
   b) deck
   c) chute

HOW DID YOU SCORE?

1	a) 0	b) 0	c) 5
2	a) 5	b) 0	c) 0
3	a) 0	b) 5	c) 0
4	a) 0	b) 0	c) 5
5	a) 5	b) 0	c) 0
6	a) 5	b) 0	c) 0
7	a) 0	b) 5	c) 0
8	a) 0	b) 0	c) 5

Total:

25-40: You really know your stuff. You've got the look
And definitely have a handle on the lingo and your riding
is coming on too.

15-25: While you know some of the buzz words, there
are certain areas where you come a bit unstuck. Let's
hope you don't get left out in the cold when it comes to
surf speak.

0-15: You're in a bit of trouble. You wouldn't know what
to say if a top rider offered to show you around back
country. Better swat up a bit or you could lose.

5 Up keep

It's important to look after your board, even if you rent one. There are some simple steps to ensure you get the best from your board every time you use it.

1   After a day's boarding, don't just sling your board in a bag or leave it dripping wet. Your board should be dried and checked over at the end of every day. If you keep a towel in your bag you can wipe away the moisture from your board every time you decide to leave the mountain alone for a couple of hours. This is a good habit to get into, especially if you board all season. Otherwise you could find a depressing combination of board warp and rust. This is bad news for perfect powder at the beginning of a new season.

2   If you really love your board then you should give it a professional service at least once for every two to three weeks in the snow.

Up keep

If you only go to the slopes once a year, then you would be wise to have your board serviced at the beginning and end of the season. The professionals will make sure that your board is completely dry. It will be inspected for grazes and gouges, and any necessary repairs will be made. It will then be sealed with a special wax so that it hibernates in perfect order.

Waxing and edging

Hot wax, irons, and edging files is a dangerous combination. Although waxing and edging is an important part of board maintenance, you shouldn't have a go without adult help. In fact, it's better left to the professionals completely.

The reason for waxing though is that it increases the board's speed on the snow as well as sealing the base and preventing water from getting into the board. There are different waxes for different temperatures and snow conditions. You should put storage wax on your board before you put it away for the season. Ask your instructor or at the nearest specialist shop for advice about who can do this for you.

EDGING

You will need to check the edges of your board regularly.
Stones and rocks can cause gouges to the base of the board
and ruin smooth edges and a smooth ride. Sharp edges
make the board more responsive. The bevel (angle) put on
to the edges will make your board easier to ride.

If you want the edges to hold well you will need to keep
them sharp. A board that is low on wax, has blunt edges or
scratches on the base will not only be slower on the snow
but it is hard to turn and tough to ride. Don't even think
about edging a board yourself – *always ask a professional to
do it for you!*

GOUGES

Damage to the underside of your board is fairly common
and unavoidable. But don't panic! You don't need to rush
out and buy a brand new, hot and up to the minute board
(shame!) just because you see a scar on the undercarriage.
Like before, get the professionals to sort out the problems.

Calling the professionals

Remember, the professionals have all the medicines to keep
your board fit and healthy.

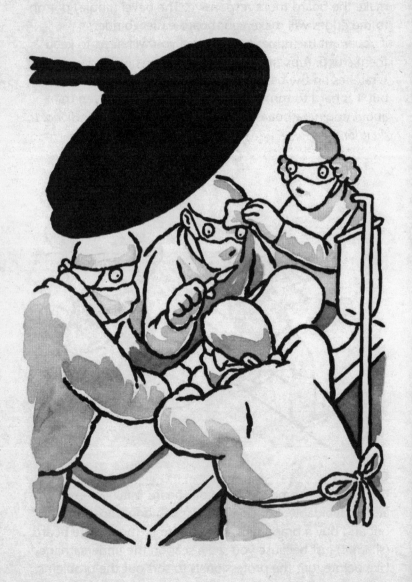

Pipes, parks and big mountains

Pipes and parks are areas created for snowboarders to learn and practise tricks and moves. A park is made up of kickers, table tops, spines, gaps and jumps made of compacted snow.

An increasing number of resorts provide "snowboard only" areas. These are sections with fun parks and half pipes, many include runs for carvers and freestylers, as well as easy flats for beginners.

Table tops

On a table top there is a take off, a landing and a top over which you jump. These are great for straight airs and grabs. Experienced riders can try spins of 180° and 360°.

Top Tip

Have you done any geometry at school? It'll impress your teacher heaps if you ask if you can have a lesson about it! And you don't even need to tell them it's to help you perfect your tricks and spins!

If you are doing a 90° turn, think of a clock. Start at the twelve and stop when you reach the three – that's 90°.

What about 180°? Think of the clock and move from twelve round to the six. That's half of the clock face or half an hour.

A 270° turn would be the same as 45 minutes on the clock. So you'd start at twelve and finish at nine.

Can you guess what a 360° is? Yup, it's all the way round the clock.

A 540° would be one and a half hours. A 720° would be two hours on the clock.

Gaps

Gaps are like big boxes with a space or "gap" instead of a flat surface. To make a successful jump you will definitely need some speed or you will miss the landing and fall down the gap. Not cool!

Spine

A spine is a ridge between two transitions on which you can practise tricks.

Pipe

A pipe is just what it sounds like: a hollow pipe or a shaped slope, like a pipe cut in half or a quarter. The best way to start is by riding as smoothly as possible across the curved area (transition) to get a feel for the pipe.

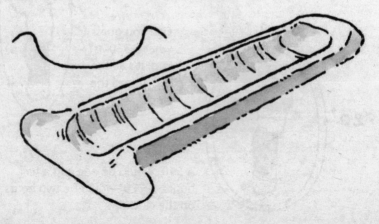

As soon as you feel confident enough, try riding to the top of the wall before turning round to jump down again. When you've got this covered, you're ready to take some air. Increase your speed, get some air and try a grab. (See the next chapter for more stuff about this.)

Park fun

Resorts are trying to make parks as much fun as possible by filling them with all sorts of obstacles. Some have buried cars and buses leaving only the roof exposed to leap over.

ANY MORE FARES ON TOP?

Pipes, parks and big mountains

Some resorts have pipe dragons for carving out a pipe, although not all of them are maintained. If you ask at the lift hut, you might be able to borrow a spade and carve out a pipe yourself.

Park etiquette

Parks and pipes are great fun but only if you follow the unwritten rules:

1 Remember to wear pads, guards and a helmet.

2 Stay clear of landing areas, unless you're the one trying to land!

3 Don't forget your pipe and park courtesy. Wait your turn.

4 Watch out for other riders.

5 Never cut ledges or steps in the walls.

6 If you fall during a run, move out of the way as quickly as possible before the next rider enters the pipe.

Rules of the slopes

Most of safe snowboarding is common sense, but there are a few things you should know before you hit the hills. The main thing is to remember that despite the fact that you've never had so much fun in your life than when you're riding, you must always remember that snowboards aren't toys, but rather highly technical pieces or sports equipment. Here are some basic rules for riding safely and happily.

1 BE AWARE

Remember there are lots of different types of people on the mountain – as well as skiers, there are telemark skiers, alpine skiers, mono skiers, beginners and freestyle snowboarders and even walkers in some places. Always be aware of other people using the mountain, and be able to anticipate the kind of moves they will make.

2 STOPPING

Always stop on the side of the slope, safely out of the way and out of danger. Never stop below a jump or a ski run turn or at the junction of two runs. Don't stop on or near jumps and always move away after you've completed your jump.

3 GET A LEAD

Never snowboard without a lead (or leash) safely secured to your front foot.

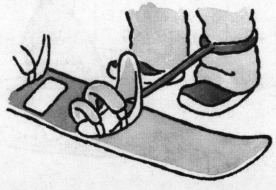

4 ACCIDENTS

If you see an accident you must stop and help in any way possible. In avalanche areas, it is also a good idea to wear an avalanche bleeper, especially when you are going off piste.

5 READ THE SIGNS

Signs warning danger such as 'avalanche danger', 'double black diamond run' or 'danger' aren't just there for fun. Make sure you read them and watch out!

7 Getting tricky!

Now you're really getting there. Your snowboard feels so much like an extension of your body that getting round without it feels odd. You can do basic moves, ollies, nollies, and jumps with no problems at all. So now it's time to add some extra bits to your ride. It's time to perfect your skills and maybe even invent some moves and tricks of your own with some mates.

"Jenny, you've gone to bed with your Board on again!"

Top Tip

As you improve your snowboarding technique, watch pro snowboarders and copy their moves. You could even get out some videos and watch some skilled tricks in slow motion to work out how to do them for yourself.

The snowboarders guide to what's hot and what's not

WHAT'S HOT

- off-piste powder
- blue skies and sunshine
- Special Blend boarding trousers
- energy drinks
- chocolate
- waiting your turn on jumps

WHAT'S NOT

- pistes crammed with skiers
- bum bags
- Coke
- chewing gum
- pushing in on lifts and jumps
- lift queues

BUM BAG

Styling it!

Freestyle is all about pulling off skateboard-style tricks on the mountain. This could be using rails, benches and boxes in the snowboard park or just creating jumps of your own or using natural jumps or moguls on the slopes. Whatever you do, if you want to show off and session like this, you've definitely got the jib-bonking urge!

Once you've perfected these techniques, you can move off to the half-pipe to really show off. Freestyle has a language all of its own, and a lot of it is borrowed from skateboarding speak.

IN A SPIN!

The first thing to learn about is spinning. You can spin forwards (spinning frontside) or backwards (spinning backside).

Spinning frontside: is turning the same way you would for a heelside turn (clockwise for goofies and counterclockwise for regulars).

Spinning backwise: is turning the same way you would for a toeside turn (clockwise for regulars and counter clockwise for goofies).

Getting tricky!

TO SPIN

1   Start with a 360° toeside turn but keep turning the board all the way up the slope. When your board stops, get your bearings. Now flatten your board and look in the direction of your spin and push your front foot in that direction.

2   Choose a good clear run with no lumps and practise spinning 360° all the way down the hill. Start off slowly or you'll be falling over and feeling dizzy!

80

MANUALS

We all know how to do wheelies on our bikes, but here's a beat trick that takes the bike to the mountain. Snowboard wheelies are wicked, especially if you do them properly right in front of a big crowd of bored-looking skiers. Here's how: Lean right back on your board and pull the tip up off the snow. Just like a bike, the better you get, the longer you'll be up in the air.

NOSE BLUNT SLIDE

Once you're comfortable doing wheelies, you can turn them sideways and slide over the snow moguls or cat tricks balancing on the edge of your board. Here's how you do it: Slide your board sideways, put your weight on your front leg and pull your back leg up so that you end up sliding on the front third of your board with the tail in the air.

There are lots of other skills, like kicking up snow with your board just like a surfer does with waves that you can try. And why not make up some of your own moves? You can even give them a name a watch to see if they catch on.

Getting tricky!

NOSE AND TAIL ROLLS

No, we're not talking about a dodgy new burger! Nose and tail rolls are when you spin 180° from either end of your board.

For a nose roll, put your weight over your front leg, and then straighten your front leg, and pull your back leg up.
Now slide your board 180° frontside to backwise so that you end up riding fakie.

Board bites

Tail rolls are the other way round. They start fakie and end forward.

Going up

If getting big air is what snowboarding is really about for you, then here are some standard moves that you'll want to perfect. A lot of these moves can be adapted to do in the half-pipe.

AIR TO FAKIE

An air to fakie starts off riding forward and turns into a fakie with a 180° spin. Start by riding across the fall line on your up hill edge, jump and throw your back foot around in front of you. Make sure you keep looking in the same direction during the tricks to keep your balance.

Board bites

One trick that got its name from its skilled inventor is the Caballerial named after the mega pro skateboarder Steven Caballero. The snowboarding version of the trick is a 180° jump that starts spinning front side and ends riding forward.

Going all the way

If you're feeling really confident, you could try taking a deep breath, saying goodbye to your pet goldfish and give your younger brother your CD collection and trying the big one. The 360° is a complete spin in the air so that your body spins and lands smoothly enough for you to ride away coolly. Wow!

"WOW!"

Board bites

You can even spin 540° and 720° when you get really good. Some of the top riders can throw 900° and still land the board. Phew! That's really something to see.

BONING

Whenever you straighten out a leg it's called boning. If you straighten out your front leg, it's called a nose bone and your back leg is a tail bone. Boning is a good trick to learn because it makes sessioning the half-pipe tricks easier.

Obstacle course

Years ago, snowboarders would have avoided logs, hand rails and benches because they would have done terrible damage to their boards. But today, with technologically superior boards and special snowboard parks, there are lots of things you can ride and have fun on without damaging your board. Best of all you can hit anything you like in the park and you won't get chased or booked by the police. Here are some of the rail grind moves you can try. Rail grinding means riding along railings or hand rails and edges of tables or benches.

85

50/50: The snowboard rides parallel with the rail grinding under the base of the board.

Board Slide: Here the rail is half way between your feet and your board is across the rail. You should grind the rail with the backside edge with your front edge in the air.

Nose slide:
Here the rail is
between your
front foot and
the nose.

Riding the half-pipe

If you're really serious about catching air, there's no better place to do this than in the half-pipe. Half-pipes used to be little more that gouged out ravines, but today they're built with specialised half-pipe tools to standardized specifications. Riders and mountain staff keep the pipes smooth every day and remove any snow that might have fallen.

The first time you go into the pipe, you'll probably wish you hadn't. You'll feel exhilarated and petrified at the same time. Don't let all those photos of guys in half-pipes in the magazines fool you! Riding the half-pipe is very hard, so you'll need to take it step by step. Try something easy first and then build up your confidence.

87

Getting tricky!

TRAVERSES

The best way to start is to practise traversing or crossing the pipe from side to side. Start by side-slipping into the top of the pipe and take a deep breath. Now let yourself go and gently ride half a metre or so up the first wall. Then turn your head and cross fakie to the opposite wall. Keep riding back and forth until you get the hang of it.

SIDE TURNS

The next stage is to practise approaching one wall on one edge and leaving the opposite edge. This is really important to get right or you won't be able to do more advanced 'core' factor tricks. Here's how: start off by side-slipping into the pipe and traversing forward to one of the walls. Ride on your uphill edge as you traverse across the flat. As you approach the peak of the vertical, get ready to turn. Pretend you're a surfer riding up a wave and turning back down. Extend your legs and turn your board back down. Then repeat the movement.

BUNNY HOPS

Now you're ready to try your first air in the half pipe. A bunny hop is basically turning in the air instead of skidding at the top of the half pipe wall. Always start practising in a half pipe without too much vertical wall to get the hang of the movement. When you get to the top of the ascent add a little hop just big enough to get you in the air.

Getting serious

If you've mastered the previous moves, then now you're ready to get serious! A lot of the moves that you learnt in freestyle, such as 360s, different grabs and cabalerials, can be used in the half-pipe. On the next page you'll find the beanie guide to half-pipe tricks. Two beanies = difficult, Three beanies = very difficult, Four beanies = virtually impossible, Five or more beanies = are you mad?

Board bites

When half-pipe first started, people were amazed by grabless airs and spins. Today, the crowd is a lot harder to please. If you can combine two or three trick moves in one, you're going to get respect. The hardest of all is something like a 720 inverted mute grab.

Alley oop: This is a 180° air where instead of turning back down the pipe as you normally would, you spin up the pipe in the reverse direction.

Two beanies

360 air to fakie: This is like the freestyle version except that in the pipe you're forced to land fakie. This is hard until you get the hang of it.

Three beanies

Caballerial: The half-pipe version of this is a 360 air which starts fakie and ends forward.

Three beanies

540s: These start and end riding forward. You've got to really commit to this trick because it's very hard to get all the way round three times. You'll end up with some spectacular bruises.

Four beanies

720s: Unless you can spin like a yoyo, leave this one to the pros!

Eight beanies

Board bites

Top snowboarder Bear Agushi from Australia was disqualified from a Big Air competition in 1995 when he pulled a Switch 900 instead of a Switch 720!

Grabbing

We already know there are lots of different grabs. But they can all be split into five basic moves:

1 Bring your knees up.
2 Reach down and grab the board.
3 Let go of the board.
4 Extend your legs to reach for the landing.
5 Bend your knees to take the landing.

Getting tricky!

Here are some other moves to get to grabs with!

Frontside air: As you leave the lip of the half-pipe, grab your toe edge between your toes with your back hand.

Crail: Grab the toe edge near the nose with your back hand.

Lien air: A frontside trick where you grab the board with your front hand on the heel edge.

Slob air: Grab the toe edge near the nose with your front hand.

Stiffies: Grab the toe side edge between your bindings with either hand straightening both legs while grabbing.

Stale fish: This top trick takes your back arm around the back of your back leg so you grab the heelside edge between your bindings.

Backside tricks

The backside air gets
you ready for tricks on
the backside wall.
Jump off the backside
wall and turn 180
degrees back into the
pipe by looking at the
spot where you want
to land. When you feel
comfortable, grab the
heel edge near the
nose with your front
hand. Here are some
other moves to learn:

Method air: Grab your heel edge between your heels with
your front hand while the board is tweaked to a table top
position parallel to the deck of the pipe.

Mute air: Grab the toe edge with your front hand between
your toes.

Indy air: Your back
hand grabs the toe
edge between your
toes.

Fresh fish: First, grab
the heel edge with your
back hand between
your heels. At the same
time, bone out your
back leg. Keep your
other arm straight to
counterbalance
everything.

Getting tricky!

Handplants, inverts and aerials

By using the same momentum that shot you out of the pipe, you can get your board over your head and your hands on the lip of the half-pipe. Now you're getting into some really advanced tricks that are only for serious boarders and pros.

If you are mad enough, the easiest move to learn is the two-handed invert. These let you use both arms to support and control your handstand. Here's how you do it:

1 Approach the backside wall in a low position with your knees bent and as fast as possible.
2 As you speed up the wall to the lip, let your board fly upwards. Land your hands on the lip while you're upside down.
3 As you drop back into the pipe, rotate your body so that it is under you again and push off the snow with your hands.
4 Make sure your body is centred over the board for landing.

LAIDBACK AIR

Here the handplant is done with one hand on the frontside wall. Ride up the wall on your toe edge. As your front foot passes the lip, reach back and plant your back hand on the lip. Your board will shoot up over your head. Now let your board fall back into the pipe.

ANDRECHT

This move gets its name from the skateboarder Dave Andrecht who invented it. It's done on the backside wall and you should start off as if you are going to do a two-handed invert but do your handstand on your trailing hand while grabbing the board with your leading hand around the front leg but in between your legs.

Tip: If you bone out your front leg, this becomes a Sad Andrecht. If you plant your front hand instead of your back hand and grab with your back hand it's an Eggplant. Got it? Good!

Pro talk

Just occasionally a snowboarder invents a new trick by accident. "I was out snowboarding and wanted to learn a handplant. I went up the front side wall, instead of the backside wall and flew upside down and round and landed back on my feet. I'd done a 540 backflip handplant without even knowing it! My friends were pretty impressed and one of them called it the Jacoby Terror Air – the J Tea for short."

Mike Jacoby, champion US half-pipe rider

Free-riding

Now it's time to get out of the pipe and back to the mountain! The whole mountain: where you can ride stuff like powder, ice, crust and crud, steeps and chutes, cliffs, and through trees – in fact anything you want to.

POWDER MONKEYS

Once you're mastered riding the piste where the snow is groomed and packed soft, it's time to go off-piste for a real adventure. The snow off-piste is powder. Riding powder is probably the best feeling you'll get and every snowboarder's dream. It's much easier to ride in powder on a snowboard than on skis because you only have one plank of wood to worry about and control, rather than two. There is no better feeling than carving turns through completely fresh snow. The trick with powder is to keep your speed up and your weight slightly back. If you slow down, you'll sink!

Pro talk

"Powder is floating. Powder is surfing."

Ben White, Snowboarder and owner of Esprit d'Equipe

Top Tip

It takes less effort to turn in powder. You need to bounce through the turns and tilt slightly from one edge to the other. Get some rhythm into your turns.

Powder safety tips

- Never snowboard in powder on your own. Make sure you can see your friends and fellow boarders at all times.

- Always tell an adult where you are going and what time you expect to be back.

- When you start, look for snow which is about a boot deep. Any deeper and it'll be more of a slog than fun.

- Watch out for hidden hazards such as tree dips and exposed rocks.

- Always be careful of areas prone to avalances. Check before you go off piste with the ski patrol for any dangerous areas, and always wear an avalanche bleeper if you are going off piste.

- Take a guide whenever possible.

Some experienced snowboarders love off-piste riding through trees. This can be great fun, but is also quite dangerous. One wrong move and you could be hugging a tree!

In the bumps

Picture this: A field of rounded bumps as tall as cars. The natural instinct for any boarder would be to turn and run for something smoother and flatter, but there are some crazy boarders who love this type of mountain roller coaster. To them, this means FUN.

Getting tricky!

There are several ways to approach these moguls. The best way for beginners is to pick a route down the fall line in between the bumps. For your first go, always pick a gentle rather than a steep slope. Approach it in a powerful, aggressive stance with your back hand forward. Keep your knees bent to absorb the shock. Your body should act like a spring-loaded shock absorber.

Keep your head level and hands forward with your knees bent to absorb the bumps.

Going extreme

When you look at all the snowboarding magazines in the shops, you'll see amazing shots of boarders leaping over cliffs as if they can fly, and turning jumps where below them is a death-defying drop. What we see in the photos makes this end of the sport look easy. But what we can't see is the hours of planning and careful consideration that went on before a jump. Nor do we see the bumps, bruises and broken limbs when the jump goes wrong.

This is the extreme end of snowboarding where the going is really tough and the boarders make life and death decisions with only their wits and ability to rely on.

Board bites

There is a World Extreme Championship held every year in remote and challenging places like Alaska.

CLIFF DROPS

For a successful cliff drop the landing must be steep, fairly smooth and soft. The run-out (the flat area at the bottom of the slope) must be long enough to prevent the rider hitting anything. The rider also needs to build up enough speed to clear any rocks.

CHUTES

These are sheer drops or narrow gulleys from the top of the mountain to the bottom. They are very dangerous. The steeper and narrower the chute, the longer the run at the bottom needs to be for the rider to slow down.

Avalanches

Avalanches are set off if layers of snow are disturbed, causing heavy slabs of snow to hurtle down the mountain. They are more likely to happen on steep slopes after a heavy snowfall.

Avalanches are very dangerous – especially at warmer times of the year when snow is melting. Off-piste riders always carry avalanche bleepers that transmit a signal that can be picked up if there is an avalanche. By following these signals, rescuers know where to find stranded riders.

So you want to be a pro?

The dream ...

Anyone who's ever boarded must have dreamt of winning big competitions and being paid by big sponsors to do the sport they love all year round with all the money they need, free equipment and gear and their pictures in glossy magazines. Snowboard heaven! But of course, only a very few riders make it to this level and you'll find out more about some of them from the profiles in this chapter.

Most of the top riders are sponsored by the big manufacturers of boarding gear: Burton, Sims, K2 and others. There are international sponsors and some that sponsor home-grown stars. There are sponsors for every part of the gear, from sunglasses to socks!

Sponsorship works by the sponsor providing the rider with money in order to pay for his travel and other expenses while he or she is competing in tournaments and championships around the world. In return, the rider wears the sponsor's products and uses their gear, promotes them and appears in adverts and videos.

Need a sponsor?

Get seen out and about on the slopes – and make sure you are the hottest thing there! You'll need to be seen riding in the big name resorts, taking part in open competitions, and even inventing new moves. You could send off videos to companies and write to magazines, sending them photographs of tricks you have done. Manufacturers do send out scouts to look for the latest, hottest, up and coming stars.

JOHAN OLOFSSON

Born: October 1976

Home: Gallivere, Sweden

Years riding: 10

Hobbies: Mountian biking, basketball, surfinf and roller hockey

In two years you've gone from twin-tip freestyle rider to an all-mountain big terrain rider. How did you do it?

"I got back to my roots."

What advice would you give to someone wanting to ride in danger zones, where avalanches could strike at any time?

"To respect 'closed' signs in resorts ... Never be alone and check the conditions before you drop in ... Just be safe, so you can do the same thing tomorrow."

How are the levels of freeriding and freestyle being pushed out?

"It's peaking. Riders are taking it to new levels in their own way. I'm lucky because I have time to progress. Some sponsors are making their riders shoot every day, leaving no time for fooling around. that's sad."

Major competition results:

Grand Prix Champion 1996

You could also contact your local snowboarding shop and ask if they will sponsor you. Look in magazines for the names of manufacturers in your country and write to them, sending photographs and details of where you have ridden and what you specialise in. Go to a national championship and take part as much as possible. It will be hard work but worth it when you get picked up by a sponsor!

Riding for a living

Imagine being paid to snowboard! You could get yourself a job as a representative for a snowboard holiday company, do washing up in a hotel or act as a guide or snowboard instructor at a resort. These jobs are always available and aren't hard to do. Or course, you won't be able to do this until you have left school and are old enough to travel on your own. But you could start planning what you want to do now by writing to a few ski and snowboard holiday companies and asking for details of jobs in the future. There are details of holiday companies in Want to know more? on page 118.

STEP INTO MY OFFICE !

Snowboard events

Look in the snowboard magazines for up-to-date information about the latest competitions and championships at resorts around the world – including the ones near to you! You could also contact the International Snowboard Federation, Pradlerstr 21, 6060 Innsbruck, Austria, telephone 0043 512 342834 and the Fédération International du Ski, Biochenstrasses 2, CH-3653 Oberhofen/Thunersee, Switzerland, telephone +41 (033) 2446161.

KENJI ISHIKAWA

Born: July 1971

Home: Asahikawa-Shi Hokkaido, Japan

Years riding: 8

Hobbies: Sleep, science fiction

Do you do any sports to help your riding?

"I'm doing yoga, which helps me to stay flexible and focused."

Major competition results:

JSBA Serious Overall Half-pipe Champion 1997

BEAR AGUSHI

Born: April 1975

Home: Melbourne, Australia

Years riding: 8

Hobbies: Building and jumping off kickers with his mates.

Major competition results:

Swatch Boardercross 1997 Champion
Australian Universities Half-pipe Champion 1996

The British National Snowboarding Championships

This is the biggest UK competition held each year in Europe. This competition is open to any British snowboarder who wants to have a go. Usually about 200 riders take part in the series of qualifying rounds.

World Ski and Snowboard Championship

This is North America's largest winter sports event that takes place in April every year, with 2,500 competitors taking part in skiing and snowboarding events. There is a knock-out half-pipe competition called the Big Air, demo events and slope style fashion shows, as well as downhill, slalom and free-style events.

US Open Snowboarding Championship

This takes place every year, and is the premier US Snowboarding event, with competitors taking part from all over the world.

World championships

There are two other main world competitions that take place every year. One is run by FIS or the Fédération Internationale du Ski, and the other by the International Snowboard Federation although the ISF event is far more respected by snowboarders. These are world class events that only top seeded snowboarders who have competeed in knock-out or qualifier rounds can take part in. They are held in different resorts every year.

British dry slope championships

You don't need snow to win prizes! Every year the Dry Slope Championships take part at dry slopes in the UK. These are open to all comers. You can contact your local dry slope for details. A list of UK dry ski slopes is at the back of the book.

World extreme snowboard championships

For the really daring, there are the World Extreme Championhips held every year in Alaska. This is open to all-comers, but only really experienced free riders take part. Competitors perform death-defying jumps from cliff tops and rock faces which they reach by helicopter.

Olympic snowboarding

Snowboarding was in the Olympics for the first time in 1998. There are six different snowboarding events: Giant Slalom (GS), Parallel Slalom, Super Giant Slalom, Snowboardercross (BX) and Half-pipe. In the Winter Olympics, held in Nagano, Japan, only two events were represented: the Giant Slalom and the Half-pipe.

WHAT'S THE GIANT SLALOM THEN?

This is similar to a downhill ski race. There are gates set up down the hill and the object of the race is to go as fast as you can around the gates. Each rider has two attempts and their fastest time is taken. If you miss a gate you are disqualified. The winner of the event is the rider with the fastest time.

So you want to be a pro?

AND WHAT'S THE HALF-PIPE?

You already know that the half-pipe is a trench-shaped like a U which is covered in compacted snow. Snowboarders perform tricks down the half-pipe and are judged by each of the five judges on basic moves, spins, flips, technical merit, landing, and how high they do their tricks.

BRYAN IGUCHI

Born: September 1973

Home: California, USA

Years riding: 8

Hobbies: Ice hockey, mountain biking, surfing, watercolour painting, breakdancing and playing guitar

Who are some of your favourite sports stars?

Carl Lewis, Matt Hoffman, Pete Sampras, Monica Seles

Major competition result:

Insbruck Extreme Half-pipe Champion 1996 and 1997

Swiss Master Champion 1995 and 1998

Sloping off

If you thought snowboarding was just about winter, Christmas trees, and cold days in woolly hats and jumpers, you were wrong! The good news for berserk boarders is that you can ride all year round.

Switzerland

Switzerland is popular with the rich and famous. But you don't need to be rich or famous board in one of the many resorts. The conditions for snowboarding are very impressive: steeps, powder, long wide pistes, pipes, parks, boardercross circuits and areas for beginners.

Swiss resorts offer modern, express lifts and the public facilities and buildings are more modern. They are also excellent for half-pipes. The bad news is that Switzerland is expensive and you'll need to speak French, Swiss or German. The good news is that some of the runs are 5+ kilometres long! There is winter riding between October to May, summer riding between May to September.

The United States

America is perfect for budget boarders – the resorts are large and affordable with loads of choice. Due to the competition between the resorts, the customer service and facilities are outstanding. There is amazing annual snowfall and even high tech snow-making machines if the snow fall is low. The winter riding season is from October to May, and then in May the summer riding starts and it ends in July. Everything is so cheap that you should take an empty case and a full wallet! Remember though that you have to tip for everything. The States are very strict about safety rules and you may be asked to attach a lead (or leash as they say) to your board. They may also insist that your back foot is unclipped when you ride the lift.

Australia

Although the Australian resorts don't match up to the facilities offered in the States, Canada and Europe, the Australian snowboarding scene is very friendly and laid back. There is often top instruction here as people come from all over the world to snowboard here when there own seasons at home have finished. The riding here is from June to October and the mountains aren't massive but the terrain is great and offers good powder.

Andorra

This is a small province of Spain located in the Pyrenees. The slopes aren't as good as some other parts of Europe, but there is a great effort to provide good resort facilities and the views from the impressive mountains are spectacular. Having said that, a week in Androrra would be too long and not challenging enough for an experienced rider. But there is a lot of flat terrain that is perfect for beginners.

Canada

The home of 270 resorts, Canada is BIG! It's one of the best countries in the world to ride off-piste powder but you'll need to pack your warmest thermal clothes because the temperatures can be freezing. Some of the lift systems are ageing and slow but as there are plenty of resorts to choose from, you could easily check this out before you go. The winter riding is from October to May when the summer riding starts and continues until September – so you can snowboard all year round! Canada isn't as cheap as America but the sense of space makes up for this. Don't forget that they speak French in Quebec!

Austria

Some people reckon that Austria is the European home of snowboarding. The Austrians encouraged snowboarding in their resorts long before other countries decided to welcome the sport. The resorts offer some long steeps which are not quite as scary as in the French Alps. You'll find lots of fun parks and pipes in Austrian resorts and riding is all year round because the winter season runs from October to May and the summer season from May to September.

France

France is a snowboarder's dream. It has some of the best snowboard resorts in the world and without doubt some of the most extreme. Whatever you want to do, the French resorts offer something for every one. Some are ugly but with great terrain. Others are slick and modern or basic and simple. There is terrain to suit every level and style of rider and snowboarding all year round. You can find cheap accomodation in France along with cheap, fast food, and cheap places to hand out. But beware of the loads of skiers who head for the French resorts!

Germany

Germany might not be up to the same opportunities as its neighbours but it still offers great terrain. With the biggest snowboarding population in Europe, Germany produces many of the best riders on the world circuit. The resorts are efficient and have great public transport systems. With winter riding from October to April and summer riding from May to July, the German resorts can cater for beginners as well as advanced riders.

United Kingdom

Snowboarding the UK is made possible by the man-made slopes and the natural snow in Scotland, where all the resorts are. Unfortunately though the Scottish snow cannot be guaranteed and the riding season is really only from January to April.

Italy

A great country with cheap boarding although they do lag behind the rest of the European resorts in the fun park and pipe department. There's riding all year round but be careful: during the holidays and weekends, the Italians hit the slopes in droves!

117

Want to know more?

Useful addresses • Websites • Mags

USEFUL ORGANISATIONS

Alaska Freeriding Federation
AFFI, 8320 Resurrection Drive, Anchorage, Alaska 99504.
Telephone 907 333 4998

British Snowboarding Association
First Floor, Trinity Square, Llandudno LL30 2PX, UK
Telephone 01492 872540

ISF Europe
Burgerstrasse 17-11, A-6020 Innsbruck, Austria.
Telephone 43 512 563890

ISF N. America
PO Box 477, Vail, CO 81658 USA
Telephone 303 949 5673

New South Wales Snowboarding Association
22 Battle Street, Balmain, 2042, New South Wales, Australia
Telephone 02 8185047

SNOWBOARD PARKS AND DRY SKI SLOPES

The Snowdome
Leisure Island, River Drive, Tamworth, Staffs B79 7ND, UK
Telephone 01827 67905
The best place to learn on real snow in the UK. It's a
specialist snow park where you can have lessons and meet
other snowboarders. There are weekly snowboard nights
with full instruction and ramps and a new quarter pipe.
There's gear for sale and masses of advice from the
professionals on site. Make a trip there — it's worth it!

Bowles Outdoor Centre

Tunbridge Wells, Kent. Telephone 01892 665665
Skiing and snowboarding, residential and non-residential
courses.

Plymouth Ski Centre

Telephone 01752 600220
Has the largest tobogan run in the UK.

Scottish Norwegian Ski School

Aviemore. Telephone 01479 810656

Southampton Ski School

Telephone 01703 790970

Swansea Outdoor Pursuit Centre

Telephone 01792 403333

Wycombe Summit Limited

High Wycombe, Bucks. Telephone 01494 474711
Large main slope, Scandinavian log cabins and 70 acres of
woodland.

SNOWBOARD HOLIDAYS

Here are some of the best companies that specialise in
snowboarding holidays. Most ski resorts offer snowboarding
instruction, including group lessons, private lessons and
specialised camps. Contact your nearest snowboarding
association (see page 118) for a list of the best places.

Chalet Snowboard Limited

31 Aldworth Avenue, Wantage, Oxon OX12 7EJ, UK
Telephone 012350767182

Mount Hood Snowboard Camp

4457 SE Wynnwood Drive, Hillsboro, OR 97123 USA
Telephone (800) 247 5552

Surf Mountain

16 Chiswick High Road, London W1 1PU, UK

Telephone 0181 994 6769

SPONSORING COMPANIES

Here's a list of the top companies who sponsor riders:

Burton Snowboards

80 Industrial Parkway, Burlington, VT 05401, USA

Telephone 802 86204500

K2 Snowboards

19215 Vashon Highway SW Vashon Island, WA 98070, USA

Telephone 800 972 4038

Sims Sports Inc

22105 23rd Drive South East, Mill Creek, Washington 98021, USA

Telephone 425 951 2700

CYBER-RIDE

Check out these internet sites for information about boarding. There's loads of new sites appearing every month and lots that gets updated, so you use your search engine to search for snowboarding and see what you can come up with. Most of the big manufacturers have their own sites too which can give you lots of information and details of gear and equipment. Just type in 'snowboarding' and have a top surf!

Mountain E-Zine: Live reports on snowboarding events and contests can be found at **www.mountainzone.com**. There are even photographs of boarders.

Snowboard Klinik: Tips on caring for your board can be found on **www.klinik.co.uk**

http://www.cccd.edu/ski.html Gives information about resorts and weather conditions in the USA.

http://www.earth.ox.ac.uk/ This is basically a clearing house for information on the net about snowboarding.

www.snow.co.nz Here you'll find information on snowboarding in New Zealand, as well as events and snow reports.

www.boarderzone.com Information about world-wide snowboarding.

www.ISF.com Check out news from the International Snowboard Federation, including Junior World Championships, rider profiles, events and a snowboarding calendar.

www.CBS.com See snowboarding as it happens at the sports news site.

The official International Snowboard Federation can be found at **www.isf.net** with lots of info, including a virtual link.

www.fmz.com is a useful site for snowboards, videos and fashion items.

Need more information about your favourite snowboard company? Try **thriveon line.aol.com** then go to **outdoors/snow/links.boards** for the snowboarding manufacturers websites.

Snowboard Designs and Outside SurfGear have joined together to provide hardcore snowboarding apparel to true snowboarders at **www.snosurf.com**

Ravensports presents an area for snowboarders at **www.ravsports.com**

READ ALL ABOUT IT

There are lots of snowboarding magazines on offer on the shelves. They're a brilliant way of keep up with what's hot and what's going on in the world of snowboarding and riders. They'll give you the low-down on the latest equipment, tell you about the best places to ride, give you the inside track on the business and the riders. There are letters, interviews with pros and reports from competitions, as well as step-by-step guides to new, hot tricks. And of course, they're crammed with fabulous colour photographs of snowboarding. Here's a selection from the magazine rack:

Snowboarder Magazine

An American magazine that is worth seeking out. Phone 717 496 5922 for more information.

Transworld Snowboarding

The top selling magazine on offer, again from the USA. Lots of photographs and loads of ads. Phone 619 745 2809 for more information.

Whitelines Magazine

The top UK snowboarding mag and it's really good. If you want to get one magazine regularly, this is the one you should go for. It'll give you all the latest from the UK and world scenes. Telephone 01235 536229 for more information.

Snowboard UK

Another top UK mag. Phone 01562 827744 for more information.

Universal Snowboard Guide

This is available from most good snowboard shops. It gets regularly updated and is the snowboard bible for finding out the best places to ride. It gives guides to all the slopes and the best places to go off-piste for powder monkeys.

Glossary

Air	A jump
Base	The underside of the snowboard
Beanie	A woollen or fleece hat
Binding	An attachment which secures the boot to the board
Bleeper	A transmitter that sends out a signal that can be picked up by an avalanche receiver
Bonk	To hit something with the base of your board while in the air
Bumps	Raised areas in the snow, also known as moguls
Button	A type of lift with a button seat that takes you up a slope
Carve	A high-speed turn where the board stays on an edge
Corn snow	This is powder that has thawed and refrozen
Dendex	A plastic material used for dry ski slopes
Edge	The side of the board which comes in contact with the snow
Extreme	A sport which involves danger. Extreme snowboarding is snowboarding in the most dangerous areas
Fakie	Riding backwards
Fall-line	The direct route straight down the mountain
Free-riding	Snowboarding style which includes all the styles

Free-style	A snowboarding style where you do jumps and tricks and ride the half-pipe
Goofy	Snowboarding with your right foot forward
Grab	Styles for tricks where you move your arms and legs
Granular snow	Caused when the powder thaws, freezes again and the surface gets hard
Half-pipe	A half pipe shaped channel carved out in the snowhard
Heel-edge	The edge of the board on your heel-side
Lip	The upper edge of the half-pipe
Nose	The front of the board
Moguls	Bumps on steeper slopes
Off-piste	Places that are not marked resort trails slopes or piste
Ollieing	A leap into the air without using a jump
Park	An area for boarders with jumps and obstacles
Piste	The marked slopes and runs that are patrolled and monitored by the resort
Powder snow	Looks like icing sugar. Good for beginners as it is the softest to land on
Racing	Snowboarding against the clock
Regular	Riding with your left foot forwards
Switch	Performing a trick backwards or fakie
Toe-edge	The edge of the board on your toe side
Wet snow	Sticky snow which makes it hard to do tricks and turns. Great for making snowmen!

Index

360 air to fakie 90
50/50 86
540s 90
720s 90

aerials 94
Agushi, Bear 108
air to fakie 83
alley oop 90
Andorra 115
Andrecht, Dave 95
Australia 115
Austria 116
Avalanche 9103

basic riding position 33
bindings 21-22, 34
board maintenance 65-68
board safety 30 (see also 46)
board slide 86
boards 18-20, 36
boning 85
bonking 62
boots 21
bunny hops 89
Burton Carpenter, Jake 10

Caballerial 83, 90
Caballero, Steven 83
Canada 116
carving it 56-57
championships 109-111
chutes 102
cliff tops 102
crail 92

dry slopes 25, 118

edging 67
exercises 37-38, 41-43, 48-59

faking 61
fall line 51
falling 35
falling leaf exercise 42
France 116
free-riding 96
fresh fish 92
freestyle 78
frog hopping 37
frontside air 92

gaps 72
gear 13-15, 24
Germany 117
giant slalom 111
goofy 32
gouges 67
grabbing 91

half-pipe 83, 85, 90
half turns 43
hand plants 94
heel anchors 26
heelside turn 38, 50
holidays 113-117, 119-120

Iguchi, Bryan 108
indy air 92
instructors 29
inverts 94
Ishikawa, Kenji 108
Italy 117

layedback air 95
lessons 27-28
lien air 92
lifts 44-45

magazines 122
method air 92
mute air 92

nose blunt dive 81
nose rolls 82
nose slide 86

ollieing 59
Olofsson, Johan 106

park etiquette 74
parks 73, 118-119
pipe 72
Poppen, Sherman 9
powder 97-99
powerstrap 26
pro info 106, 108, 112
pro talk 11, 39, 51, 55, 62, 80, 96, 97

quizzes 40, 63

resorts 114-117
rules of the slope 75-76

side turns 88
sideslips 41
Sims, Tom 9
skiing 11, 12, 29
slob air 92
snowboarding associations 118
snowboarding, types of 16-17
snowboards 18-19
spine 72
spinning 79-80
sponsorship 105-107
stale fish 92
standing up 38
stiffies 92
stomp pads 26
sunsense 15, 26
switching 61
Switzerland 114

table tops 70
tail rolls 82
toe-side turns 38, 49
traverses 88
traversing 42
turns 48-50, 52-55

United Kingdom 117
United States 114

walking the board 37
warming up 31
waxing 66
websites 120-121

ACTIVATORS

All you need to know

0 340 715162	Astronomy	£3.99	☐
0 340 715197	Ballet	£3.99	☐
0 340 736305	Basketball	£3.99	☐
0 340 715847	Birdwatching	£3.99	☐
0 340 715189	Cartooning	£3.99	☐
0 340 736496	Chess	£3.99	☐
0 340 715200	Computers Unlimited	£3.99	☐
0 340 736275	Cricket	£3.99	☐
0 340 715111	Cycling	£3.99	☐
0 340 715219	Drawing	£3.99	☐
0 340 736313	Film-making	£3.99	☐
0 340 736291	Fishing	£3.99	☐
0 340 715138	Football	£3.99	☐
0 340 736321	In-line Skating	£3.99	☐
0 340 715146	The Internet	£3.99	☐
0 340 736267	Memory Workout	£3.99	☐
0 340 715170	Riding	£3.99	☐
0 340 736518	Rugby	£3.99	☐
0 340 715235	Skateboarding	£3.99	☐
0 340 736526	Snowboarding	£3.99	☐
0 340 71512X	Swimming	£3.99	☐
0 340 73650X	Your Own Website	£3.99	☐

Turn the page to find out how to order these books

more info • more tips • more fun!

ORDER FORM

Books in the Activators series are available at your local bookshop, or can be ordered direct from the publisher. A complete list of titles is given on the previous page. Just tick the titles you would like and complete the details below. Prices and availability are subject to change without prior notice.

Please enclose a cheque or postal order made payable to Bookpoint Ltd, and send to: Hodder Children's Books, Cash Sales Dept, Bookpoint, 39 Milton Park, Abingdon, Oxon OX14 4TD. Email address: orders@bookpoint.co.uk.

If you would prefer to pay by credit card, our call centre team would be delighted to take your order by telephone. Our direct line is 01235 400414 (lines open 9.00 am – 6.00 pm, Monday to Saturday; 24-hour message answering service). Alternatively you can send a fax on 01235 400454.

Title .... First name .... Surname ....

Address ....

....

....

Daytime tel .... Postcode ....

If you would prefer to post a credit card order, please complete the following.

Please debit my Visa/Access/Diner's Card/American Express (delete as applicable) card number:

Signature .... Expiry Date ....

If you would NOT like to receive further information on our products, please tick ☐ .